THE SECRET OF THE SCORPION-EATING MEERKATS ... AND MORE!

BY ANA MARÍA RODRÍGUEZ

★ANIMAL SECRETS REVEALED!★

Enslow Publishing
101 W. 23rd Street
Suite 240
New York, NY 10011
USA

enslow.com

Acknowledgments
The author expresses her immense gratitude to all the scientists who
have contributed to the Animal Secrets Revealed! series. Their comments and
photos have been invaluable to the creation of these books.

Published in 2018 by Enslow Publishing, LLC.
101 W. 23rd Street, Suite 240, New York, NY 10011

Library of Congress Cataloging-in-Publication Data
Names: Rodriguez, Ana Maria, 1958- author.
Title: The secret of the scorpion-eating meerkats... and more! / Ana María
  Rodríguez.
Description: New York : Enslow Publishing, 2018. | Series: Animal secrets
  revealed! | Includes bibliographical references and index. | Audience:
  Grades 3 to 6.
Identifiers: LCCN 2017004625| ISBN 9780766086272 (library bound) | ISBN
  9780766088481 (pbk.) | ISBN 9780766088429 (6 pack)
Subjects: LCSH: Mammals—Behavior—Juvenile literature. |
  Mammals—Behavior—Research—Juvenile literature.
Classification: LCC QL739.3 .R63 2017 | DDC 599.15—dc23
LC record available at https://lccn.loc.gov/2017004625

Printed in the United States of America

To Our Readers: We have done our best to make sure all websites in this book were active and appropriate when we went to press. However, the author and the publisher have no control over and assume no liability for the material available on those websites or on any websites they may link to. Any comments or suggestions can be sent by email to customerservice@enslow.com.

Photo Credits: Cover Aaron Amat/Shutterstock.com; pp. 3 (top right), 13 Stefanie Van Der Vinden/Dreamstime.com; pp. 3 (center left), 18 Steffen Foerster/Dreamstime.com; pp. 3 (bottom left), 26 Matthewgsimpson/Dreamstime.com; pp. 3 (bottom right), 33 Egon Zitter/Dreamstime.com; pp. 3 (top left), 9 Gwolters/Dreamstime.com; p. 6 Mauro Rodrigues/Dreamstime.com; p. 7 Wrangel/Dreamstime.com; p. 8 Alex Thornton; p. 12 Gerald Mothes/Dreamstime.com; p. 16 Ronnie Epstein/Dreamstime.com; pp. 19, 20 Lydia Luncz; p. 25 Youri Mahieu/Dreamstime.com; p. 31 Patrick Rolands/Dreamstime.com; p. 35 Amy V. Smith and the lab group at the University of Sussex, in the Mammal Vocal Communication and Cognition Research Group; p. 37 Canettistock/Dreamstime.com; p. 40 Cvijun/Shutterstock.com.

★ CONTENTS ★

★

ENTER THE WORLD OF ANIMAL SECRETS

In this volume of Animal Secrets Revealed!, you will travel to the African Kalahari Desert to attend meerkat survival school. Your next trip will take you to California, where hyenas get the highest grades in tests of intelligence. Then, you will travel to scorching-hot Brazil, where capuchin monkeys do something scientists thought only humans could do. Back in Africa, scientists uncover chimpanzees' eating habits by looking at their bones and hair. Finally, horses reveal the secret of how they know human emotions.

Welcome to the world of animal secrets!

1
MEERKATS GO TO SURVIVAL SCHOOL

A hungry meerkat pup blurts out begging calls. An adult meerkat responds by bringing the pup a dead scorpion. It is bigger than the pup's head! The pup does not hesitate. It takes the scorpion in its mouth and munches on it slowly.

A large bird called a yellow-billed hornbill sees the pup eating the scorpion and gets closer to it. The hornbill yanks the scorpion, but the pup does not let go. The bird takes flight, lifting the scorpion and the meerkat with it. The hornbill lunges and plunges, but the pup holds on. Finally, 5 feet (1.5 meters) above the ground, the pup lets go of the scorpion. The young meerkat hits the desert floor, unharmed.[1] Indeed, life is not easy for meerkat pups living in the African Kalahari Desert!

Scorpions raise their tail when they feel danger. Notice the sharp poisonous stinger at the end of the tail.

Studying Meerkats in the Wild

Scorpions are one of meerkats' favorite foods, even though scorpions have a poisonous stringer on the tip of their tails. Some scorpions have enough poison to kill an adult person. Meerkats, however, do not seem discouraged by the deadly prey.[2]

British scientists Alex Thornton and Katherine McAuliffe were curious about how meerkats learn to catch such a poisonous prey without being stung. They traveled to an area in the Kalahari Desert where meerkats are used to people. For a meerkat in that area, a person is just like another big animal in the desert, like an antelope. Meerkats being comfortable around people allowed Thornton and McAuliffe to get close enough to observe the animals' activities without disturbing them.

"We woke up early in the morning to study meerkats," says Thornton. "Some days they were easy to find, while other days they were nowhere to be found. We had to be patient if we wanted to understand how meerkats go about their day."

Meerkat helpers take good care of their young. They watch what the babies are doing and listen to their calls.

Meerkats live in groups of up to forty individuals. Those that are older than ninety days, called helpers, work together to raise the younger ones.

"Pups are initially incapable of finding their own prey," says Thornton.[3] So, they make loud begging calls. Thornton and McAuliffe saw that the helpers did not simply feed the pups when they begged for food. It seemed that something more was going on.

How to Hunt Scorpions

To catch a scorpion, an adult meerkat searches under the sand. How a meerkat finds a scorpion, however, is still a mystery. It could be that a meerkat smells the scorpion, feels its movements in the sand, or uses another sense.[4]

Where is the Kalahari Desert?
The Kalahari is a desert in southern Africa, mostly in Botswana. It also covers parts of Namibia and South Africa.

When a meerkat locates a scorpion, it quickly digs it out of the sand and swats it on the head and pincers. The meerkat has to do this quickly, before the scorpion has a chance to sting its predator. Then, the meerkat catches its prey, usually by the tail.

Scorpion-Hunting Lessons

As Thornton and McAuliffe observed the Kalahari meerkats, they realized that the animals do not learn to catch scorpions on their own. The helpers give scorpion-hunting lessons to the pups.

School is on! A meerkat helper watches a young meerkat practicing a scorpion-eating lesson.

Lesson 1: How to Eat a Dead Scorpion

The first lesson introduces scorpion food to young meerkats. A hungry four-week-old meerkat pup raises a racket of begging

Meerkat family members care for each other by working in teams.

calls. In response, a helper kills a scorpion and brings it to the pup. To encourage the pup to eat, the helper nudges the dead scorpion toward the pup.

As pups get older, they get better at handling and eating dead scorpions. They change their calls, which is a clue for helpers to move on to lesson 2.

Lesson 2: How to Eat a Live, Stingless Scorpion
The second lesson encourages young meerkats to practice handling

Science Tongue Twister
The scientific name of the meerkat is *Suricata suricatta.*

TEACHING VERSUS COPYING

Scientists know that some young animals learn from older animals of their own kind. What is hard to tell is whether the adult is teaching the young animal or the young one learns by copying the adult. Meerkats are the first mammals, other than humans, known to teach their young. Some ants and birds called pied babblers also teach skills to others of their kind.[5]

and eating live, stingless scorpions. A helper catches a scorpion, bites off the poisonous stinger, and gives the live, stingless scorpion to the pup. If the scorpion escapes, the helper catches it and gives it back to the pup.

When the pups approach ninety days old, they are ready for lesson 3, the final lesson that will test their survival skills.

Lesson 3: How to Eat a Live Scorpion with a Stinger

A helper catches a scorpion and brings it alive, stinger and all, to the pup.

Thornton and McAuliffe observed hundreds of meerkats go through survival school. They concluded that the more the pups practice handling scorpions in lessons 1 and 2, the better they will do in lesson 3.

Thornton and McAuliffe discovered one of the secrets of the meerkats' survival in the wild. Meerkats give paws-on lessons to their young about how to catch and eat scorpions without being killed by the deadly prey.[6]

2
GO TEAM HYENA!

Christine Drea, an expert in animal behavior, calls two of her spotted hyenas by name to do an experiment. The experiment would show whether hyenas cooperate with each other to solve a problem. The hyenas have lived all their lives in captivity at the Field Station for Behavioral Research at the University of California, Berkeley. Although they are familiar with their enclosure, they refuse to enter the room Drea has set up for the experiment.

"My colleague Allisa Carter and I had installed something new to the hyenas in this room. A metal platform 2.7 yards (2.5 meters) above the ground with two ropes hanging from it," says Drea.[1]

On top of the platform, the scientists had placed two bone chips the size of small pork chops and two meatballs. To get the food, which the hyenas could smell from the ground, one animal had to pull from one of the ropes at the same time that the other pulled from the other rope. Drea and Carter wanted to know whether hyenas that had never done this before would be able to figure out that the only way to get the food was by cooperating with each other.[2]

Spotted hyenas line up, getting ready to hunt in their natural habitat.

Despite Drea calling them by name, the hyenas did not want to go into the room that had a contraption with which they were not familiar. This reaction was not surprising. Scientists know that hyenas are wary of new things in their natural environment. They say hyenas are neophobic, or have a fear of new things.

Hyenas form close-knit packs to keep an eye out for predators such as lions and prey such as zebras.

"It took the hyenas several weeks to get used to having the platform in this room," says Drea. "We had to be patient and wait until they willingly entered the room to do the experiment."[3]

Hyenas Are Fascinating Animals

Hyenas in the wild live in groups called clans, each led by a top-ranking female, the matriarch. The clan is a family. Together, hyena family members defend their territory, hunt for food, and raise and protect their young.

To carry on these activities, scientists thought, hyenas had to be able to coordinate their strategies. However, nobody had done experiments to test that hyenas were team players. Instead, scientists had studied cooperation in primates such as chimpanzees. They chose primates because they do intelligent things, such as make and use tools. If they can make tools, then maybe they also can work as a team.

Interestingly, primates do not cooperate in experiments for getting food as much as scientists expected. Actually, this supports what scientists see in nature, where primates seldom work in organized parties to get food.[4]

Hyenas are a different story. Hyenas do work together in the wild to get food. Although they do scavenge, some hyenas hunt most of their food. Scientists have seen hyena clans use highly organized tactics to target and bring down prey that is usually larger than the hyenas are.

> **Science Tongue Twister**
> The scientific name of the hyena is *Crocuta crocuta*.

"A spotted hyena has to rely on another spotted hyena to bring down certain prey," says Drea. "Their survival depends on it."[5]

Drea and Carter decided to do experiments to test the hyenas' teamwork.

Pull on That Rope!

Once the hyenas at the field station accepted the platform in the room, Drea and Carter challenged the animals in pairs. The scientists set up the food on top of the platform, let the two ropes hang, and called two hyenas into the room.

"We filmed their behavior and timed how long it would take for them to figure out that they had to pull the ropes at the same time to get the food to come down to the floor," says Drea.[6]

The hyenas had not done this test before, so the scientists expected that it might take them some time to figure it out. Not at all.

"The first pair walked into the room and solved the puzzle in less than two minutes. My jaw literally dropped!" says Drea.[7]

In a similar experiment, chimpanzees were often disorganized and took much longer to complete the task.

"Hyenas are more hardwired for social cooperation than chimpanzees," says Drea.[8]

HYENA STYLE

Having Fun with a Rope, Hyena Style

One day, Christine Drea walked into the room with the platform and could not believe her eyes. "We put the ropes up on the platform when we finish an experiment. Somehow, one of the ropes had slipped down and was hanging from the contraption," says Drea. "A hyena was biting on the rope with its teeth and swinging limply back and forth. It looked like it was playing the hyena pendulum game! It was funny to me that a fully grown hyena, a top predator in the wild, was just hanging from the rope like a huge sausage. Several weeks back, the hyena did not even want to enter the room. Now it was totally comfortable with the contraption and having fun with it."[9]

Hyenas get together to reinforce their family bonding.

Drea and Carter confirmed this result with many other pairs of hyenas. Hyenas quickly figure out how to work together to get the food reward. The results of these and other experiments have revealed some of the hyenas' secrets.

"Hyenas do pay attention to other members of their clan," says Drea. "They have strategies to work together and solve problems quickly and efficiently; that is in a well-organized way. They are very smart animals indeed!"[10]

3

THE SURPRISING ROCK-SMASHING HABITS OF CAPUCHIN MONKEYS

t is summer at Serra da Capivara National Park in Brazil, and the heat is unbearable. Lydia Luncz and Michael Haslam, primate scientists from the United Kingdom, have come to the park to study capuchin monkeys in their natural environment. The British scientists and their Brazilian colleagues want to learn more about how capuchins use tools to open nuts they like to eat.

"The capuchins are well adapted to the heat and dryness of their habitat, but it was difficult for me and my colleagues to follow the monkeys under a blasting sun, heat above 104 degrees

Capuchin monkeys are naturally curious about their surroundings.

Fahrenheit (40 degrees Celsius), and extremely dry weather," says Luncz. "It was hard for me because I live in England and we don't see the sun very often. I also had to watch for scorpions on the ground. It took a while to get used to working under these conditions, but we all managed to do it."[1]

Despite the extreme climate, the scientists followed the monkeys for several weeks as the animals went about their daily activities.

"We find the monkeys easily because during the summer time there is no rainfall at all and the monkeys go down to the water holes," says Luncz. "We observe them and follow them most of the day as they leap from tree to tree, chitchat, climb on tall boulders, and use stones as tools. Sometimes the monkeys climb up very sharp cliffs and it is not very easy for a person to follow. We make videos and speak up on top of the video to describe what we see. We take pictures and a lot of notes."[2]

Lydia Luncz watches a capuchin monkey perched in a tree.

The scientists wanted to observe closely how the monkeys choose stones and use them to crack nuts open. They were surprised to discover that the capuchin use of stones had an unexpected result.

Capuchin Monkeys Are Master Stone Smiths

Capuchin monkeys in Brazil's Serra da Capivara National Park are one of the best "handymen" in the wild. They use stones as tools in more ways than any other monkey. They use them as hammers to pound open hard nuts. They turn them into shovels to dig out spiders from the ground. Female capuchin monkeys even use stones to attract males. They throw stones at a potential mate to catch his attention.

The capuchins at Serra da Capivara are also the only ones scientists have seen pounding one stone directly against

Lydia Luncz sets her video camera to record the capuchin's activities. Notice one monkey in the background.

another with the intention of damaging the stones. A monkey holds a rounded stone with one or two hands and pounds it forcefully and repeatedly against a rock on the ground. Then, the monkey sniffs or licks the rock crushed on the ground. Scientists still do not know why capuchins do this. They speculate that the monkeys may get something from the rocks that is helpful to them, like nutrients or medicine.[3]

Unexpected Discovery
One day, Luncz, Haslam, and their colleagues were attentively observing capuchin monkeys smashing rocks on top of a boulder.

"The rock-smashing and licking was all very interesting, but what fascinated us was the broken pieces that they made," says Luncz. "We picked up the small broken pieces that were falling on the ground below the boulder. It blew our minds away to see the pieces were shaped like flakes with sharp edges. They looked just like the first stone tools human ancestors made two million years ago!"[4]

Although the scientists saw capuchins make many stone flakes as they smashed one rock against another, they never saw the monkeys using the stone flakes as cutting tools.

"The capuchins do not make stone flakes on purpose," says Luncz. "The flakes are a consequence of their everyday behavior."[5]

The scientists realized that this unexpected discovery was very important because up until then, humans were the only ones known to make these sharp-edged stone flakes. Luncz, Haslam, and their colleagues changed their project from observing capuchins using rocks to open nuts to how they make stone flakes.

"We focused on this capuchin behavior," says Luncz. "We collected more stone flakes from the ground, and watched and videotaped the monkeys. We also gathered more stone flakes by excavating underneath boulders where capuchins smashed rocks. Then, we went back to our laboratory in England with a bag full of stones flakes and other rocks."[6] The scientists brought the stone flakes to Tomos Proffitt, an expert in ancient human tools.

FUNNY MONKEY

Lydia Luncz has a lot of fun while studying capuchin monkeys. She says, "They have very distinct personalities. There is the playful one, the quiet one, the bully. It's like watching a soap opera every day; it's so much going on! We had a little one that got used to us very quickly. No other capuchin would dare do what he did. He would quietly come and steal nuts out of our pockets. Sometimes we would not even notice it until we saw him running away with the treat."[8]

"I was pretty gobsmacked," says Proffitt. "I have learned how to make these things. I was looking at this material and it looked like it had been made by humans."[7]

It took many months for Proffitt and other colleagues to study the capuchin-made stone flakes and compare them with ancient human-made tools.

Stone Flakes Tell a Story

Proffitt used the same technological analyses he had used when studying ancient human tools, and his own experience making stone tools, to study the capuchin-made stone flakes. He uncovered exactly how the stones broke. He figured out which piece came out first and which one came off next. By looking at the pieces under a microscope, he could see where a stone had been hit, because the hit creates a mark. The microscope revealed how each stone flake ended up in the shape the scientists found it.[9]

"We can practically see the behavior of the monkey in the stone," says Luncz. "We can say that the monkey must have turned the rock this way, then he must have hit it this way, and, after that, he turned it this way and hit it this way. We can read a stone like a book and know what happened to it."[10]

All these analyses and tests revealed that capuchin monkeys make stone flakes that are no different from those made by the first human ancestors. Scientists thought that only humans and their ancestors were able to create these types of tools. The secret is out! Capuchin monkeys can unintentionally make them, too.[11]

4
SOME CHIMPS LIKE MEAT ON THEIR PLATES

It is morning at Tai National Park. Located in Ivory Coast, the park is home to chimpanzees living in one of the rain forests on the western coast of Africa. On this humid morning, a party of six chimpanzees quietly walks on the forest floor in the direction of noisy calls made by red colobus monkeys. When the monkeys see the chimpanzees approaching, they become louder, raising a racket of alarm calls. Working as a team, the chimpanzees launch an attack on the red colobus.

Chimpanzees walk together, preparing for a hunt.

The colobus, fearing for their lives, scramble in all directions. They try to put distance between themselves and the chimpanzees throughout the canopy of 31-yard (28-m) tall trees. More often than not, the chimpanzees succeed and catch their prey.[1]

Scientists know this because they have followed and observed the chimpanzees during their hunting trips. The alpha male chimpanzee leads the group to a successful hunt. Then, the group shares the meat according to what each chimpanzee has contributed to the hunt.

What Chimpanzees Eat

Chimpanzees eat mostly fruits and nuts. However, after watching them hunt, scientists realized that some chimpanzees like to add meat to their plates. Studying chimpanzees in the wild is not an easy task. Primatologists, scientists that study primates such as chimpanzees, follow the animals constantly as they explore the rain forest looking for prey. It is hard to get close enough without disturbing them to see how much meat they actually eat and how often.[2]

Two red colobus monkeys in a tree watch attentively for any sign of danger. Some chimpanzees like to add this monkey meat to their diet.

Scientists know that some chimpanzees are better hunters than others. But does that mean that better hunters eat more meat? Geraldine Fahy and colleagues decided to work together to answer the question.

Fahy is a biological anthropologist. She studies how people, their culture, and society have evolved, or changed over time. Chimpanzees and people have some things in common. For instance, both hunt. Studying hunting in chimpanzees can shed some light on how human societies that no longer exist used to hunt.

To answer the question of how much meat chimpanzees eat, Fahy did not join her primatologist colleagues watching what chimpanzees do in the forest. She stayed in the laboratory and studied the animal's bones and hair instead.[3]

"You Are What You Eat"

Fahy and her colleagues worked as a team. She asked the primatologists to bring her samples of

NITROGEN IN TISSUES

How to Measure the Amount of Nitrogen in Tissues

Geraldine Fahy used a laboratory technique called stable isotope analysis to measure the amount of nitrogen in chimpanzees' bones. She needed only a small sample of bone; about what would fit on top of an American quarter (about 1 inch, or 2.5 centimeters, in diameter). Fahy treated the bone sample with chemicals to separate collagen from the other components of the bone. Then, she prepared collagen samples to measure the amount of nitrogen with a mass spectrometer. She also used a similar procedure to measure nitrogen on pieces of hair 0.4 inches (1 cm) long.[4]

chimpanzee bones from the ribs and the femur, the largest bone in the leg. She also asked for hair samples.[5]

The primatologists brought skeletons and hair samples of chimps from Tai National Park

to the Max Planck Institute for Evolutionary Anthropology in Germany, where Fahy was doing the analyses. These chimpanzees had died of illness or accidents in the wild.

To figure out how much meat chimpanzees eat, Fahy looked at how much of the element nitrogen was in the animals' bones and hair. Nitrogen is an element that identifies proteins such as meat.[6]

"You are what you eat," says Fahy. "The more meat you eat, the more nitrogen will accumulate in your bones and hair."

At first, the primatologists were not convinced that studying bones and hair would add any new information about the chimpanzees' diet.

"It was a bit of a struggle at the beginning to convince them that these data would help complete the picture of what the chimps are actually eating," says Fahy. "However, at the end they realized that the nitrogen data provided information they could not get easily with observations alone."[7]

Fahy also received samples of the fruits and nuts the chimpanzees would find in their environment. She determined the amount of nitrogen in these samples, too. With all these samples at hand, Fahy proceeded to find out whether better hunters eat more meat.

Bones and Hair Reveal a Secret

Fahy compared the amount of nitrogen in the fruits and nuts with that in the chimpanzees' bones and hair. If the chimpanzees' bones and hair had similar amounts of nitrogen as the fruits and nuts, then Fahy would know that the chimpanzees were eating mostly those types of fruits and nuts. However, if the bone and hair samples had more nitrogen than the fruits and nuts, then the chimpanzees were most likely eating other foods rich in protein, such as meat.[8]

Fahy repeated her analysis a few times to make sure, and she was happy with the results. She found that better hunters had more nitrogen in their samples than the other chimpanzees.

She also found that female chimpanzees in general had less nitrogen than males. "This result matches the primatologists' observations that most females neither participate in the hunts nor have a share of the prey," says Fahy. "The exception was the best hunter's companion. She had more nitrogen in her bones than the other females. It seems that the lead hunter shares some of the meat with her."[9]

BONE VERSUS HAIR

Geraldine Fahy measured nitrogen in hair and in bone. She tested two types of bones—rib and femur—because these bones can tell what the animals ate at different times in their lives. The bone in the rib renews itself completely in about five years. Bigger bones, such as the femur, take between fifteen and twenty years to renew. By looking at the amount of nitrogen in rib bones, Fahy knew how much meat a chimpanzee had eaten during the last five years of its life. The nitrogen in the femur told her how much meat had been on a chimpanzee's plate during the last fifteen to twenty years of the animal's life.

Hair, on the other hand, can give an idea of the diet in the last six months to a year of an animal's life. Scientists think that chimpanzee hair probably grows as human hair does, about 0.4 inches (1 cm) every month.[10]

> **Science Tongue Twister**
> The scientific name of the chimpanzee is *Pan troglodytes*. Scientists call red colobus monkeys *Procolobus badius*.

By combining laboratory work with observations in the field, Fahy and her colleagues now have a better picture of what chimpanzees do with the meat they hunt. The best hunters eat more meat than the other chimpanzees in the hunting party. Females, who usually do not participate in the hunt, do not put meat on their plates. The companion of the lead hunter, however, gets part of his share of the hunt.

Chimps get together in groups to bond and communicate. Scientists discovered that the best hunters eat more meat than other chimpanzees in the group.

Fahy and other scientists can also use her work to reveal other animal secrets. Her work has shown that measuring the amount of nitrogen in bones and hair is a reliable way to have an idea of what chimpanzees eat. Therefore, scientists can apply her technique to study the eating habits of chimpanzees that scientists have not followed in the wild. By collecting bones and hair and analyzing the amount of nitrogen, scientists can calculate how much meat chimpanzees eat. Then, scientists could expand and confirm these findings by observing chimpanzees in the wild.[11]

Not All Chimpanzee Groups Hunt the Same Way

The chimpanzees in Tai National Park hunt for meat as a group. In other areas, however, scientists have seen single chimpanzees hunting alone. There are still many secrets to uncover about chimpanzee lifestyles and habits. Scientists are continually looking for new ways to reveal their secrets.[12]

5

A HORSE'S SECRET: HOW THEY KNOW PEOPLE'S EMOTIONS

In the dark hour of the early morning, Amy V. Smith and her colleagues walk toward stables in Sussex, in the United Kingdom. They are carrying several video cameras, tripods, and large photographs of men with angry or happy faces.

"Other people visiting the stables gave us a funny look," says Smith. "They didn't know that we were setting up the equipment to do experiments with horses. We wanted to know whether horses read human emotions."[1]

Horses look at each other's faces often. Scientists think this may be a form of communication.

Smith studies animal behavior. Since she was a young girl, Smith has been interested in how animals interact with people.

"I grew up in a house with lots of pets," says Smith. "I got familiar with horses when I stayed at a farm in Southern Ireland during the summer months. Animals are very good at communicating their emotions. For instance, you can tell when a dog is angry because it bares his teeth. You can tell it is happy because it wags its tail and nuzzles your arm."[2]

People can understand animal emotions. But can animals understand ours? Smith suspected that this was possible, in particular with horses.

"I wanted to work with horses because they can sense the emotions of their herd mates," says Smith. "Also, people often say that horses are good at reading human emotions. This is a reason why horses are good therapy partners of people who struggle with their physical or mental health."[3]

Before Smith planned her experiments with the horses, she searched the library for works similar to what she wanted to do. She wanted to know whether other scientists had already explored the question. She found work with dogs that showed that they do respond to human faces expressing emotions. Dogs turn their head to the right and gaze with the left eye to look at angry faces. They do not change their gaze when they look at a happy face. Surprisingly, Smith did not find much scientific work on this topic about horses.

Excited about studying something nobody had explored before, Smith and her colleagues then decided to carry out a series of experiments. They would visit stables in Sussex and Surrey and test the horses' responses to happy and angry human faces.

How to Know Whether Horses Read People's Faces

Early in the morning at the stables, Smith and her team walked toward the fields and gathered a few horses.

"We put their head collars on and led them to their stables. We gave them hay and water for breakfast," says Smith.[4]

In an empty stable nearby, the scientists set up the video cameras and brought in one horse at a time. The team then

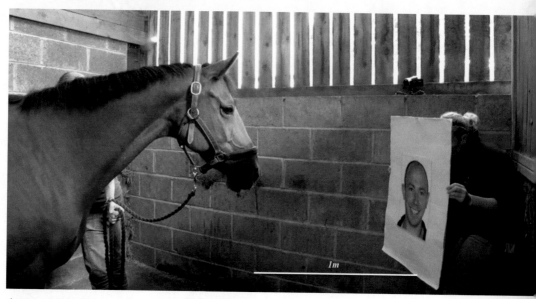

A scientist shows a horse a photo of a man's happy face as a camera on the wall films the horse's reaction.

showed each horse a large picture of a man's face and video recorded the horse's reaction. In the first group of experiments, the pictures showed a happy face. Then, the scientists showed the horses the face of an angry man.[5]

Smith and her colleagues expected that the horses would respond in a way similar to the dogs. They would turn their head to the right when looking at an angry face and would not turn their head either way when they looked at a happy face. The only way to know, however, was by doing the experiment.

In addition, the scientists attached to the horse a device that measured the animal's heart rate, or how fast the heart beats. The heart rate speeds up when an animal is facing a situation that might be scary or threatening, such as seeing an angry face.[6]

Horse Therapy
People sometimes use horse-assisted therapy to help improve their health or other conditions. Accompanied by a therapist and a horse handler, the person receiving therapy interacts with a horse in several ways. For instance, the person can just pet the horse, feed it, walk by it, or ride it.

Happy Face Versus Angry Face

Smith and her colleagues returned to their laboratory carrying the videos of the sessions with the horses. They looked at the videos many times and recorded their observations. To make fair observations of the horses' responses to the pictures, the scientists that looked at the videos did not know whether the horse was seeing a happy face or an angry face. Scientists call this being "blind" to part of the experiment. Two members of the team independently and blindly described the reactions of the horses. Later, they compared their descriptions.

A boy and a horse connect; the boy offers food while the horse looks in the direction of the boy's face.

The team of scientists was pleased to see that the two scientists had independently recorded the same results. The horses turned their head to the right and gazed at the picture with their left eye when they were looking at an angry face. However, they did not turn their head either right or left when they were looking at a happy face. This is similar to what dogs do in similar situations.[7]

The heart rate measurements backed up the video recordings. The horses' heart rate increased more when the animals were looking at an angry face than when they were looking at a happy face.

Smith and her team have uncovered a secret of horses. They are the first ones to show scientifically that horses can tell the difference between a happy and an angry human face. The scientists think that during the long history of people and horses living and working together, horses have learned to read human faces. This would help

PLAYFUL HORSE

Sometimes, the horses Amy V. Smith and her colleagues worked with just wanted to play with the researchers after looking at the photos. "One of the more curious and playful ponies really liked one of our photographs, which showed a happy human face," says Smith. "At the end of the test, he took the photograph in his mouth and tried to take off with it, nibbling the researchers when we tried to get it back from him!"[8]

horses know whether a person approaching them is friend or foe. Recognizing an angry face might warn a horse of danger and allow the animal to run away.

This discovery can also help bring people and horses together. If horses can read happy and angry emotions, they might also understand other emotions. Scientists suspect that other animals, not just horses and dogs, might be able to sense how people feel by looking at their faces.

HANDS-ON ACTIVITY: SCIENCE TREKS

Sometimes, researchers travel far away from their homes to pursue their scientific explorations. Other times, they do not leave their hometown.

Where in the world did they go?
Use a copy of the map below to trace the route the research team members in each one of the chapters followed from their home country to the country where they carried out their research. (Do not write in this book!)

How many miles?
In a notebook, copy Table 1. Write the name of the country where the researchers reside and the research destination for each of the chapters in this book. Then, using an atlas or Google Maps, determine the distance in miles between the country of origin and the one where the scientists carried out their research.

How far will you travel?

If you joined the researchers, how long would your trip be?
Copy Table 2 (on page 42), and then write the name of your
home city and the research destination for the research team
of each of the chapters. Then, use an atlas or Google Maps
to determine the distance in miles from your place of origin to
each research destination.

Chapter topic	Country of origin	Country of research destination	Miles (or kilometers) between origin and destination
Chapter 1: meerkats			
Chapter 2: hyenas			
Chapter 3: capuchin monkeys			
Chapter 4: chimpanzees			
Chapter 5: horses			

Table 1

Chapter topic	Your home city	Country of research destination	Miles (or kilometers) between origin and destination
Chapter 1: meerkats			
Chapter 2: hyenas			
Chapter 3: capuchin monkeys			
Chapter 4: chimpanzees			
Chapter 5: horses			

Table 2

Questions

- Which research team traveled the farthest from their home? How many miles did they travel?
- Which team traveled the least?
- Which one was your farthest trip? How many miles (kilometers)?

★ CHAPTER NOTES ★

Chapter 1: Meerkats Go to Survival School

1. Dr. Alex Thornton, Skype interview with the author, December 19, 2016.
2. Alex Thornton and Katherine McAuliffe, "Teaching in Wild Meerkats," *Science* vol. 113, 2006, p. 227.
3. Dr. Thornton.
4. Thornton and McAuliffe, p. 228.
5. Thornton and McAuliffe, p. 229.
6. Thornton and McAuliffe, p. 228.

Chapter 2: Go Team Hyena!

1. Dr. Christine Drea, telephone interview with the author, December 21, 2016.
2. Christine Drea and Allisa Carter, "Cooperative Problem Solving in a Social Carnivore," *Animal Behavior*, vol. 78, 2009, p. 967.
3. Dr. Drea.
4. Drea and Carter, p. 968.
5. Dr. Drea.
6. Ibid.
7. Ibid.
8. Ibid.
9. Ibid.
10. Ibid.

Chapter 3: The Surprising Rock-Smashing Habits of Capuchin Monkeys

1. Dr. Lydia Luncz, Skype interview with the author, December 23, 2016.
2. Ibid.
3. Ewen Callaway, "Monkey 'Tools' Raise Questions over Human Archaeological Record," *Nature*, October 19, 2016, http://www.

nature.com/news/monkey-tools-raise-questions-over-human-archaeological-record-1.20816.

4. Dr. Luncz.

5. Ibid.

6. Ibid.

7. Callaway.

8. Dr. Luncz.

9. Tomos Proffitt, Lydia Luncz, Tiago Falótico, Eduardo Ottoni, Ignacio de la Torre, and Michael Haslam, "Wild Monkeys Flake Stone Tools," *Nature*, vol. 539, 2016, p. 85.

10. Dr. Luncz.

11. Proffitt et al.

Chapter 4: Some Chimps Like Meat on Their Plates

1. Christophe Boesch, "Cooperative Hunting in Wild Chimpanzees," *Animal Behavior*, vol. 48, 1994, p. 653.

2. Geraldine Fahy, Michael Richards, Julia Riedel, Jean-Jacques Hublin, and Christophe Boesch, "Stable Isotope Evidence of Meat Eating and Hunting Specialization in Adult Male Chimpanzees," *Proceedings of the National Academy of Sciences*, vol. 110, 2013, p. 5829.

3. Dr. Geraldine Fahy, Skype interview with the author, December 9, 2016.

4. "Isotope Analysis," PBS Time Team America, http://www.pbs.org/time-team/experience-archaeology/isotope-analysis (accessed Dec. 10, 2016).

5. Dr. Fahy.

6. Fahy et al.

7. Dr. Fahy.

8. Fahy et al.

9. Dr. Fahy.

10. Fahy et al.

11. Ibid.

12. Boesch, p. 653.

Chapter 5: A Horse's Secret: How They Know People's Emotions

1. Dr. Amy V. Smith, email interview with the author, October 28, 2016.
2. Ibid.
3. Ibid.
4. Ibid.
5. Amy V. Smith, Leanne Proops, Kate Grounds, Jennifer Wathan, and Karen McComb, "Functionally Relevant Responses to Human Facial Expressions of Emotions in the Domestic Horse (*Equus caballus*)," *Biology Letters*, vol.12, 2016, doi: 10.1098/rsbl.2015.0907.
6. Ibid.
7. Ibid.
8. Dr. Smith.

★ GLOSSARY ★

anthropology ★ The study of humankind.

clan ★ A large family or a group of families.

collagen ★ A protein found in skin and bone.

element ★ A substance that cannot be broken into another. The elements in nature are listed in the periodic table.

enclosure ★ A place closed in by a fence or another boundary.

femur ★ The longest bone in the leg.

heart rate ★ Number of heartbeats occurring during a specific time; for instance, 100 beats per minute.

isotope ★ A form of an element with a different number of neutrons in the nucleus.

mass spectrometer ★ An instrument that separates atoms and molecules according to their mass.

matriarch ★ The female who is the head of a family.

nitrogen ★ An element that is a found in protein.

pincer ★ A claw.

poison ★ A toxic substance.

predict ★ To say what will happen.

primatologist ★ A scientist who studies primates, such as chimpanzees, orangutans, and gorillas.

scavenge ★ To feed on discarded food.

speculate ★ To guess what would happen.

tactic ★ Steps followed to reach a goal.

★ FURTHER READING ★

Books

Gray, Leon. *Amazing Animal Tool-Users and Tool-Makers.*
North Mankato, MN: Capstone Press, 2015.

Gregory, Josh. *Meerkats.* New York, NY: Scholastic Press, 2016.

Hartley Edwards, Elwyn. *The Horse Encyclopedia.* New York,
NY: DK, 2016.

Shaffer, Jodi Jensen. *On the Hunt with Hyenas.* North
Mankato, MN: The Child's World, 2016.

Websites

National Geographic Kids
kids.nationalgeographic.com/animals/spotted-hyena
Learn more about the spotted hyena.

Nature Video Production
youtube.com/watch?v=j0jqJUF1nOs
Watch capuchin monkeys make stone flakes.

★ INDEX ★